BRIGHT
IDEA
BOOKS

AMANDLA
Stenberg

by Jenny Benjamin

CAPSTONE PRESS
a capstone imprint

Bright Idea Books are published by Capstone Press
1710 Roe Crest Drive, North Mankato, Minnesota 56003
www.mycapstone.com

Library of Congress Cataloging-in-Publication Data
Library of Congress Cataloging-in-Publication Data is available on the Library of Congress website.
ISBN: 978-1-5435-5789-3 (library hardcover)
978-1-5435-6034-3 (paperback)
978-1-5435-5821-0 (eBook PDF)

Editorial Credits
Editor: Claire Vanden Branden
Designer: Becky Daum
Production Specialist: Colleen McLaren

Photo Credits
Alamy: AF archive, 10–11; AP Images: Jordan Strauss/Invision, cover; iStockphoto: valentinrussanov, 30–31; Newscom: 21 Laps Entertainment/Album, 16–17, Newscom, PG/Splash News, 25; Rex Features: Dan Steinberg, 26, Rex Features, Doane Gregory/Warner Bros./Kobal, 5, Rex Features, Peter Brooker, 9, Shutterstock Images: Featureflash Photo Agency, 13; Shutterstock Images: Joe Seer, 23, 28, Shutterstock Images, Kathy Hutchins, 7, 18, Shutterstock Images, Ovidiu Hrubaru, 15, 21

Printed in the United States of America.
PA48

TABLE OF CONTENTS

CHAPTER 1

TAKING a Stand

"I think it's great for young women, especially black young women," said Amandla Stenberg. She was talking to a reporter. She was at the premiere of her latest movie. It was called *Everything, Everything*. She was proud of the movie. She played the main character, Maddy.

Stenberg has many talents. She does more than act. She also **directs** movies. She sings and writes too. But most of all she loves helping others.

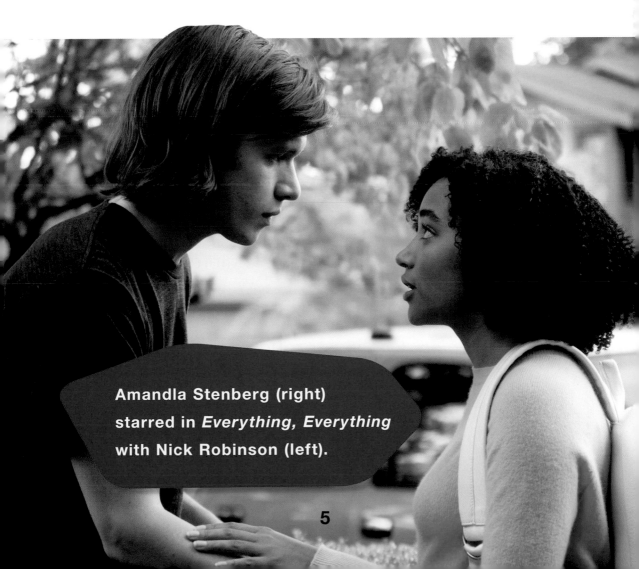

Amandla Stenberg (right) starred in *Everything, Everything* with Nick Robinson (left).

Stenberg once made a video for her history class. The video was about **cultural appropriation**. Sometimes people use something from black **culture**. They often do so without giving **credit**. She said this is wrong.

Stenberg speaks up about world problems. She stands up for others.

Stenberg isn't afraid to share her opinions.

CHAPTER 2

POWER
Actress

Stenberg was born on October 23, 1998. She is from Los Angeles, California. Her mother is African-American. Her father is white.

Stenberg started making commercials at age four. She also modeled for Disney. At school she was in musicals. She was once the fiddler in the musical *Fiddler on the Roof*.

Stenberg liked acting from an early age.

Stenberg's character's name in *Colombiana* was Cat.

BIG BREAK

Stenberg's first big break came at age 12. She acted in the movie *Colombiana*. In the movie a woman becomes a killer. She played the woman as a child.

POWER NAME

Amandla means "power" in Zulu. This is a language used in South Africa.

But an even bigger part came the next year. Stenberg played Rue in *The Hunger Games*. Then many people learned who she was.

In 2012 Stenberg was named the "Number 1 Breakout Kid Actor" by *Entertainment Weekly*.

CHAPTER 3

OTHER
Roles

The Hunger Games was a big hit. It changed Stenberg's career. Then Stenberg worked on smaller movies. One was called *As You Are*. She also acted in a TV show called *Sleepy Hollow*.

Stenberg at the premiere of *As You Are* in 2017

RIGHT FOR THE ROLE

Stenberg read *The Hunger Games* many times. She saw herself playing Rue. She believed she could get the part.

Stenberg often picks parts with a message. She acted in *Where Hands Touch*. She played a black girl in **Nazi** Germany.

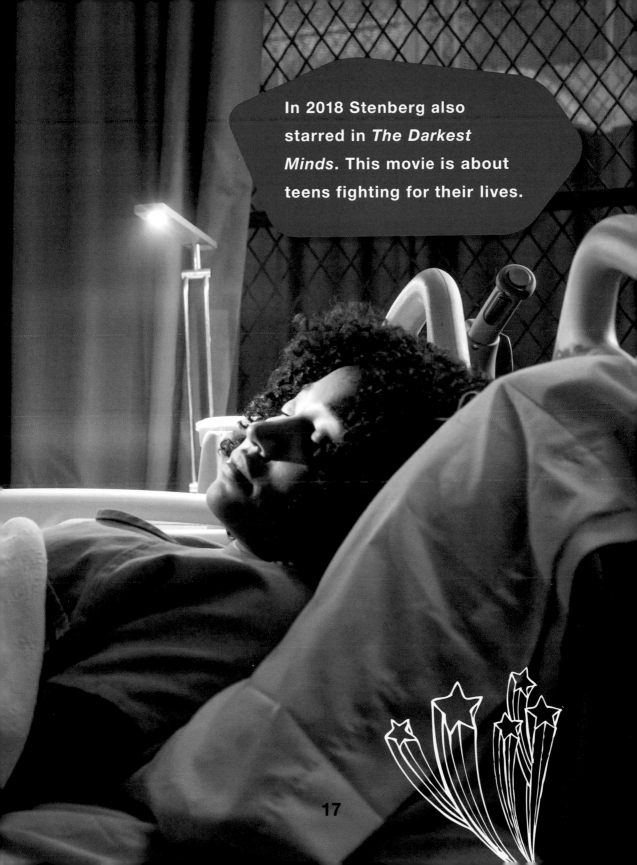

In 2018 Stenberg also starred in *The Darkest Minds*. This movie is about teens fighting for their lives.

Stenberg starred in three movies in 2018.

In 2018 Stenberg was in *The Hate U Give*. This movie is based on the book by Angie Thomas. It is about a teenage girl. She sees her friend get shot by a police officer. Stenberg played the main character. The movie is about **racism**.

CHAPTER 4

MANY
Talents

Stenberg likes to make music.

She plays the violin, guitar, and drums.

Her band Honeywater made a record

in 2015.

In 2017 Stenberg made a video for teens. It was called "You Are Here." The video helps teens with self-care.

Stenberg enjoys sharing her talents with the world.

21

Stenberg often puts her talents together. She directed and sang in a music video for *Everything, Everything*.

Writing is another talent of Stenberg's. She cowrote a comic book called *Niobe*. The main character is a black elf. The book is about love and adventure.

NIOBE

Niobe is the first comic book with a black hero, writer, and artist.

Stenberg wrote her first *Niobe* comic in 2015.

CHAPTER 5

GIVING
Back

Stenberg is young. But she works to change the world. She uses social media to spread **awareness**. She is not afraid to share her beliefs.

Stenberg speaks up about women's rights. She fights for women of color. She believes they should have more parts in movies. She also thinks there should be more black women in books.

Stenberg is often asked to speak at events about standing up for others.

Stenberg considers herself an actress and activist.

HELPING OTHERS

Stenberg also helps other causes. She works with No Kid Hungry in the United States. This group works to end child hunger. Stenberg also gives money to help schools in Africa.

Stenberg works hard for her job. She also works hard to fight for others. She knows the importance of standing up for people.

GLOSSARY

awareness
a state of being well-informed

credit
praise or acknowledgment

cultural appropriation
when someone outside another culture uses things from that culture without giving proper credit

culture
the beliefs, values, and way of life of a certain group of people

direct
to be in charge of actors and crew members for a movie

Nazi
the German hate group organized and led by Adolf Hitler before and during World War II that wanted a pure German race

racism
the belief that one race is better than another

TIMELINE

1998: Amandla Stenberg is born.

2002: Stenberg starts making commercials and modeling in catalogs.

2012: Stenberg appears in *The Hunger Games* as Rue.

2015: Stenberg makes a video for her history class to raise awareness on cultural appropriation.

2017: Stenberg stars in *Everything, Everything*.

2018: Stenberg stars in *The Hate U Give*.

ACTIVITY

BECOME AN ACTIVIST

Stenberg made a video for her history class. The video had an important message.

You can share a message that is important to you too. First, research a topic. Pick something you want to change in the world. Look up information about the topic and take notes. Think of what you want to change. Support your ideas with reasons. Find sources or examples to support your points.

The next step is to make a video like Stenberg did. Be sure you are following a script. A script tells actors or readers what to say. Your script should include your ideas and reasons. You may talk about your sources.

Last, present your movie to a group of friends. This is called a screening. Your friends will view your movie. Then they may ask you questions.

FURTHER RESOURCES

Want to learn more about Stenberg and other strong women? Read this book:

McCann, Michelle Roehm. *More Girls Who Rocked the World: Heroines from Ada Lovelace to Misty Copeland.* Hillsboro, Oregon: Beyond Words, 2017.

Ready to learn more about being creative like Amandla Stenberg? Check out these websites:

Hello Kids: Making Your Own Movie
http://www.hellokids.com/c_26899/hellokids-daily-kids-news/making-your-own-movie

Scholastic: Story Starters
http://www.scholastic.com/teachers/story-starters

INDEX